AF480753

MY UNIQUE ABILITY

ADAM JOEL SCHROEDER

Published by Spines
ISBN: 979-8-89383-477-2

CONTENTS

"THE LOST LITTLE BOY"

The lost little boy
Cries and weeps
Their must be a secret
That he has to keep

Not knowing when
He will smile again
For this little boy
Is only just ten

He shivers and moans
In all hours of the night
For this little boy
Stays up till it's light

He carries his stuff
All that he can carry
There's never enough
There's only just worry

He wants to feel hope
Instead of despair
He's trying to cope
Instead of being scared

Lost little one
Please don't cry
For someone will come
To hold you tight

I know you will feel
The sigh of relief
Instead of feeling
All of this grief

So please understand
Your time will come
Please reach out your hand
My precious dear Son

Never look back
At these moments you feared
For I have more joyous
Memories to share

During this time
In an uncaring world
It doesn't matter
If you're a boy or a girl

Just remember that I'll take you in
For you are my child
And my very best friend!

"MY UNIQUE ABILITY"

I struggle sometimes to learn
And to cope
But what I yearn for the most
Is having some hope

I need to be determined
To do the best that I can
Even if others laugh at me
No matter who I am

But sometimes I think
I can still do better
Even if I'm not as good as another

It's hard not to compare myself to you
Because of how well
You seem to get through

Because I have this disability
That keeps me from knowing

Every little thing just keeps me going

So please never doubt
What we can do
Just always remember
I'm here for you

"LONELY LITTLE BOY"

Lonely little boy
Tries to get up but he falls
Wondering if his mom will ever call

It's hard for him to make any friends
Because with him it always depends
Figuring out what he will do next
Getting a call or even a text

This lonely little boy
Reaches out when he's young
This time around he's feeling so dumb

Wondering why he feels this way
Hoping that everything will be okay

He hates being lonely
With no friends around
He whispers your name
But doesn't hear a sound

I think he'll keep trying
To stand up through it all
He will try to not let another teardrop fall

"LOOKING BACK"

Looking back at these moments I've had
Makes me very joyful and glad

I sometimes think it goes by too fast
Because memories just never last

When I ponder and when I'm there
My memories are everywhere

I will always remember when
I wish I could live these moments again

But for now they will always be
In my heart eternally

"Whispers of Mourning Dew"

Hearing whispering whispers of mourning dew
I'm very thankful that I've found you

Hearing these whispers as soft as my touch
Saying I'm grateful and that I love you so much

You are part of my dear family
Someone I need right here with me

Whispering these secrets that we have from our heart
Be thankful forever, may we never depart

"THE RIVER RUNS THROUGH"

The river runs through
Up and down, do you see it too?

Carefully observing each flow that it takes
It's movements are astounding
Every move that it makes

Quiet and gentle some parts can be
With each new experience
God's works we can see

It's enjoyable to watch when I watch with you
Every time that we see the river runs through

"WHERE IS THE FEATHER GOING?"

Where is the feather going?
Did it fall in the stream that is flowing?

Why is the feather so light?
Did you happen to see it come out of your sight?

Why didn't it land when it came to me?
There is something that is very unique

Never knowing where it will go
It might disappear moving high or low

But no matter what happens to this feather
It will always withstand any kind of weather

"WONDERING WOODS"

Wondering wood's did all it could
To supply us with needs
To help us succeed

Wondering wood's bear with me
For something wonderful just struck me

Did you happen to see what I see
These Wondering wood's are affecting me

Up and down walking along the trail
These Wondering wood's can never fail

No one can look down if they stop to see
These Wondering wood's are following me

"SUNSET SYMPATHY"

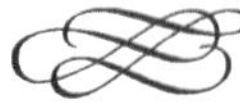

Sunset sympathy
Oh how much you mean to me

When the stars are set
When we first met
You are always there for me

Sunset sympathy
There are new ways it can set me free

To find someone
You are so proud of
Being part of your family

One big move to make it through
Sunset sympathy
I'm here for you

When you're down
I'm around

To turn your frown upside down

Never worry never fret
For we both want to see this sunset

If this lasts then we'll be
In each other's memories

"FEELINGS OF LOST HOPE"

Feelings of lost hope
Feel depressing and hard to cope

Looking down when I frown
I don't see anyone around

But when I think of this time
I always want to be kind

Waiting in patient for you to come
So I can finally see someone

For this feeling to disappear
I feel you when you are near

Coming towards me when I see you
Can help me make it through

Feelings of lost hope can never be
What my life was meant to be

So don't give up and always cope
And just get rid of these
Feelings of lost hope

"OUT OF THE RAIN"

When I step out of the rain
I will never be the same

Someone loved, someone cried
I don't want to live this lie

It's always hard to forget
Feelings that have so much regret

When I step out of the rain
This time I want my life to change

For the better when you come
I'm really glad that I've found someone

"YOUNG AT HEART"

I feel young at heart
Everyday I need a new start

Whether old or whether young
We can always meet someone

To be there when we're scared
The power of love is everywhere

We can find true friends near or far
It doesn't matter what age we are

To bind our friendship even more
We'll be best friends forevermore

"FEAR OF AGING"

Fear of aging makes me cry
Our purpose is not to die

Every moment of everyday
We need each other come what may

To face the struggle of repeated pain
This is not what I want to gain

For my patience feels so thin
We have the hope to live again

But for now my breath is sighing
That's why I have a fear of dying

"WHEN IN DOUBT"

Full of doubt just seems to be
Harder than what life was meant to be

Never knowing what things will come our way
Wondering if everything will be okay

Help me out when I'm in doubt
And show me what life's all about

I know we can be
Happy if you're here with me

Never let go of what we know
Just stay on that narrow road

If we're careful then we'll succeed
Together for eternity

"COLORING OUTSIDE THE LINES"

Coloring outside the lines
Makes me feel just fine

When things don't go my way
I just stop to think and pray

When my color turns to blue
I want to be right here for you

But when my life turns upside down
I know you'll always be around

If I draw or if I trace
I'll be happy with this place

Keep on trying then you'll be
Inside the lines for me to see

"CHILDHOOD MEMORIES"

Childhood memories
Always seem to come back to me

Flashbacks happen all the time
Whenever I recall them back to mind

It just feels like I'm not the same
I don't think I'm the one to blame

When you get older
You lose your way
My talents suffer everyday

But I try hard to find it again
Looking back when I was ten

It's just so hard when time goes fast
I know I can't live in the past

I just look forward with peace of mind
Knowing everything will be just fine

"THE WIND SOARS"

The wind soars through the door
Calling out for me to see more

Everyday it comes my way
Never knowing what to say

It stays in silent to see the effect
I look forward not looking back

Please understand this harsh wind
For I will always see it again

Up and down it breeze through trees
Wondering if it'll breeze through me

Please be careful as it comes by you
This is what you have to do

Just stand still don't hesitate
Or it might just be too late

For us to calm this wind so high
Everything will be just fine

"WHERE'S THE SANDCASTLE?"

Where's the sandcastle?
Did you find it under that thistle
Or is the sandcastle
Under your whistle?

Wherever you build it
Build it with care
For a storm may appear anywhere

If it's not strong
Something is wrong
It will not hold up for very long

But if you build it strong and firm
Then that's the lesson that I want you to learn

"WHISPERING WONDERER"

Whispering wonderer
Don't you cry
Everything will be alright

The sun went black
The stars are gone
Will love come back
Something must be wrong

Whispering Wonderer
Don't cry no more
For someone will relieve
Your pain that's torn

Whispering Wonderer
Where is your laugher
I'll take care of you
It's you I'll look after

Mending your pain

Making it disappear
I will always want to be there

Whispering Wonderer
Cry no more
I know what you're looking for

Someone to care and a friend to hug
Saying to you
I love you so much

"THE TIME I CAN'T HAVE BACK"

Looking back at
The time I can't have back

When memories gave me
The happiest that I could be

All that's left there
Is when I have them to share

In my mind and in my heart
These memories can easily fall apart

Looking back at
The time I can't have back
Wishing I was in the past

Because when we spend our time together
My happiness can last forever

Be aware

I'm in despair
Looking at these moments that I've shared

They make me happy
They make me live
I wish I could live these moments again

"I'LL NEVER SEE MY MEMORIES AGAIN"

My own mistakes
Made my heart break

When I feel my own despair
It just made me unaware

That the things I do
Can affect me and you
Every time that I see you

In my dreams
I believe my heart can mend
Cause I believe
I'll never see my memories again

Draw them out
Paint a picture
Talk them out
With each other

Again, that's when
I'll never see my memories again

"THE FLOWER AND THE PETAL"

The flower and the petal
Is all that really mattered

It once came down
And hit the ground
Lost in the wind forever

The flower and the petal
May not be made of metal

But it's beauty is seen
Through all that it means
Not one is left together

The flower and the petal
Can survive any kind of weather

It flows ever so high
It touches the sky
Until it vanishes forever

One quiet night
Just turn on the light
Look out your door
And let it in once more

"COME WITH ME"

Come with me
And you'll see
Everything that you were meant to be

Darkness holds me in it's grasp
Help me before my world collapse

Be careful when my heart subsides
Even if I start to cry

Come with me
Then I'll be
Happy for the world to see

"THE FIRE AND THE FLAME"

The fire and the flame
Will never be the same

When you blow it out
Don't talk about
Something that will make you pout

The fire and the flame
It made me feel ashamed
It once was bright
Sometime at night

Always looking for this light
To be alone without a friend
To look at them and say I'm proud of them

Wondering why we look so high
Trying to find this light at night

Pulling down our fears so low

I think I already know

Where this fire and flame can be found
I think it was always around

"DROWNING IN MY TEARS"

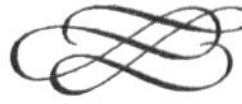

Drowning in my tears
Facing my own fears

Forever on my own
I wish I was not alone

Deep down inside
I feel my passion come alive

With every tear that falls
You help me through it all

Drowning in my tears
Facing what is near

From this I see
Who I can be
Facing my own reality

Every day I seem to struggle

Stepping in and splashing in a puddle

Look out for you
In everything we do

I'll always be your friend
A friend that's here for you!

"OH, DEAR FRIEND OF MINE"

Oh, dear friend of mine
You always are so kind

Lifting me up when you're around
Lifting my frown upside down

Giving me hope when in despair
Helping me to dry my tears

Oh, dear friend of mine
I want you to make the sun shine

Never dark, never broken
Help me with words that feel unspoken

"THE LONELY LITTLE FOSTER CHILD"

The Lonely Little Foster Child
I haven't seen you in a while

The night seems long
Something must be wrong

It's cold outside, the stars are bright
Who will tuck you in at night?

The floor seems cold from where you stand
I wish I could reach your hand

Dear foster child you sit and wait
Hoping that it won't be late

To free you from this dying fear
Hoping you find someone who cares

It's been too long just keep on trying
Somewhere there's a heart that's dying

But if this happens don't sit and fret
Look to me I'm not done yet

Because I know that true love grows
This is something that I know

Because of you little foster child
This long wait will be worth your while

When you see me and I see you
Then we'll be together me and you!

"HEAVENLY FATHER"

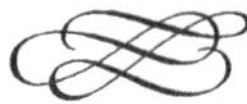

Heavenly Father I need you here
My cries for help make me run in fear

With confidence and courage
You pick me up when I fall
When I need your help
You're by my side through it all

Never knowing what will come our way
By your side is where I'll always stay

Through every new challenge
Whether big or small
My Heavenly Father you're the one I will call

"I'M NOT ALONE"

I feel lonely inside of my heart
Jehovah please help to give me a start

Guiding with comfort and deep empathy
Knowing you'll always be right here with me

Sometimes I find myself stuck with no hope
With your loving guidance you help me to cope

Pick me up Father and don't let me fall
For your Word gives comfort and help after all

This world makes me feel like I can't go on
Please help me to always be strong

We have the hope to make paradise our home
With you by my side I am never alone

"LOST LITTLE SHEEP"

Lost little sheep don't you cry
For your Heavenly Father will be by your side

Wondering and feeling with heartfelt appeal
Making Jehovah feel so real

Lost little one it'll all be okay
Just come back to Jehovah and pray everyday

These words of comfort will help us if we fall
Jehovah will teach us to stand up tall

With every decision we make if it's wrong
Rely on Jehovah, he will make you strong

Lost little sheep please don't weep
For Jehovah will be there to shepherd his sheep

With confidence and courage

Jehovah wants you back home
Lost little sheep you are never alone

"I'LL TURN TO YOU"

Please help me and comfort me
With your help, I can believe

Through these stressful times I look to you
In my heart you'll carry me through

When I'm in doubt you help me see
To face my fears and to continue to help me

My tears of pain are always long
Keep me in mind to make me strong

I feel that this is so hard for me
I need you Jehovah to strengthen me

In times of need, in times of stress
Please take care of me, and to always bless

The narrow road I safely walk on
Don't you worry, it won't be too long

Soon Jehovah will wipe all our tears
To calm our hearts and to erase our fears

One day soon we'll be in paradise
The time will come to get rid of Satan's lies

We will stand in heartfelt praise
When we see that time we'll be amazed

So don't feel discouraged and don't feel down
Jehovah our God is always around

I know that he will carry me through
When I need you the most, I'll turn to you

"BE BOLD, BE STRONG"

Be bold, be strong
Choosing what is right and wrong

We choose daily what to feed our mind
Things that are bad or things that are kind

Jehovah will help you to choose what is right
He will always be by your side

If you turn away then have no fear
For you can come back because he is near

Be bold and be strong
Jehovah will help you to conquer what's wrong

Deep inside you know what is right
For Jehovah will give you everlasting life

He knows you very well
If something is tempting he can always tell

Always look to him for courage and might
For he knows that you can win this fight

Be bold, be strong
Turn away from what is wrong

For his strength makes us bold
In his Word we're always told

To turn away from what is bad
We want to make Jehovah's heart glad

During this time of spiritual need
We need him to help us succeed

Remember Jehovah's day won't take too long
As long as we stay bold and strong!

"IF YOU PRAY"

If you pray
Jehovah will help you
If you pray
Jehovah will guide you

If you pray
Jehovah will say
Take my right hand and hold on tight
For I will give you the power and the light

So if you pray
Jehovah will teach you in so many ways
If we stand up and do what is right
He'll always be our guiding light

So if you pray every day
Jehovah will keep you in mind always
So if we pray, then we'll stay
Close to Jehovah each day

So please take courage my faithful dear friend
Jehovah will be with you right down to the end

"I TRY MY BEST"

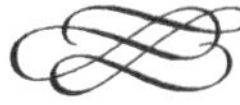

I try my best
To face each test

Every test that comes my way
For many years I often pray
To Jehovah I calmly say

There's no God I trust more than you
To give me strength and to pull me through

But things get worse in Satan's world
Jehovah is like a priceless pearl

I try my best
To look to your Word
Instead of worldly things that I've heard

Whenever I feel lonely and depressed
You take away all of my stress

Please help me to feel like I'm blessed
Because in the end I've tried my best!

"DRY YOUR EYES"

Dry your eyes
Everything will be alright

Through the darkness that we push through
Jehovah will always be with you

Through many heartfelt tears
He will be there to calm your fears

Dry your eyes
Because real soon we'll be in paradise
Even if you're strength is weak
Jehovah God will help you to speak

To others about his coming day
The dead will rise we so often pray

For many more to see the light
We will see Jehovah's might

To stand up firm in integrity
Face your fears and always see

Jehovah will be by your side every day
Dry your eyes
It'll be okay

Never knowing what's in store
Jehovah will bless you forevermore

"PROVIDE THE STRENGTH THAT I NEED"

Provide the strength that I need
I need you Jehovah to help me succeed

In this world so full of doubt
It's okay to weep and pout

But don't always feel this pain
If we preach in Jehovah's name

Be careful cause it's dangerous out there
We need Jehovah's loving care

He will take care of us
When it's dark out there

So give us the strength that we need so much
To help us in need and to feel your gentle touch

Because you love us in this time that's so hard
We know you're not very far

Please provide the strength that we need
Because we need to spiritually feed

Our brothers and sisters around the land
If we take Jehovah's hand

He will help us to make a stand
For what is right and what is true
Jehovah will always be with you!

"YOU GIVE ME COMFORT"

You give me comfort through these difficult times
Your Word fills me with hope and helps me to be kind

I know you will always be
There for me

So give me the comfort
To stand up on my knees

I beg you Jehovah with all of my heart
No matter what happens
You'll never depart

You give me such comfort when I am depressed
In a world full of trouble and a world full of stress

You know what I need to help me in life
If I look to your Word
I know what is right

I believe in you and your heartfelt desire
When I read your Word I always feel inspired

To walk along safely for I can stand
When I call on your name help me to understand

For your Word brings us comfort when things are unfair
You'll cherish and protect me under your loving care

"CHANGES"

Changes are needed to fill us with hope
In this time of trouble we need to just cope

Believe in Jehovah to change what we fear
Instead of running from a lion or even a bear

We want to have peace with all living things
Jehovah is loving, yes, peace he will bring

No matter what happens he keeps us in mind
To follow his wisdom and to always be kind

These changes are needed to keep us alive
To know that his Kingdom will arrive right on time

So be happy and give Jehovah praise from our heart
In our time of need please help us play our part

Please bring these changes that we need very soon
We stand in awe of your wonders, the sun, stars and moon

No matter what trial that we may face
Look up to Jehovah instead of this place

For he will fill the earth with peaceful delight
Instead of wickedness we will come to his light

If we believe that this will come true
Then these changes will affect me and you

"TEMPORARY"

This is our temporary home
With Jehovah we're not alone

On the outside looking in
We were born with temporary sin

The earth is filled with so much hate
We need more love this we can relate

If we stay strong and stay on the right road
We will be happy, yes, this we know

Jehovah will guide us because he cares
We will flee from Satan, always be aware

Of things that will tempt us in this dying place
Because of Jehovah, we need a happy face

To serve him forever as long as we live
This temporary home is not all that we have

For we know that we stand up in praise
For his mighty arm he will rightfully save

He'll care for us now right down to the end
For he is our Father, our God and our friend

"LONELY ONE"

Lonely one
Rise up from the dark

Lonely one
You can conquer the dark

Lonely one
Have no fear
For Jehovah your God is drawing you near

Lonely one
He will take you in
As a loving Father and a generous friend

Lonely one
Always look ahead
For Jehovah will be able to awaken the dead

Lonely one
There is no need to cry

For Jehovah our God will be by your side

Through all of these troublesome times
He will make you happy, not just sometimes
For if you stay strong and never give in
Then lonely one you'll always have a friend

"ALWAYS REJOICE"

Always rejoice
And sing with your voice

For Jehovah will help you
In all that you do

For when we were young our lives are what matters
For if we stand firm all wars he will shatter

Always rejoice
And sing loud with our voice

Jehovah will be beside us no matter what
For in Daniel's day the lion's mouth's he shut

So stand up and see
What we can believe
For Jehovah will hold on firm our sighs of relief

Always rejoice in him we can trust
Jehovah knows that we are just dust

For if we believe and trust in him
He will help us right down to the end

"NEVER LET GO"

Never let go
Of things that you know

Things that you need
And help you to see

Never let go
Of things that you trust
Always obey for this is a must

Never let go
Of things that are near
For Jehovah will get rid of your fear

Never let go
When life gets you down
For Jehovah himself is always around

He'll follow you closely

For this I must say
Never let go
And trust in him always

"WE HAVE HOPE"

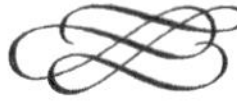

We have hope
That helps us to cope

In these hard times
We struggle to survive

But if we stand tall
We will conquer it all

We have hope
To battle our fears
To have tender love
That comes from above

No matter what happens to us in this life
Jehovah will give us everlasting life

To rise from darkness to rise from despair
Jehovah our God will always take care

Of things that will bless
And to get rid of all stress

So if we have hope
Then he can help you to cope

"FORGIVE FROM THE HEART"

Forgive from the heart
And do not keep holding on
To things that cause pain
And to things that are wrong

Keep loving each other
Please don't let me down
Jehovah will hear us
For he's always around

Forgive from the heart
So we can depart
These feelings inside of us
Will cause a big fuss

We never want our family to feel this way
So pray to Jehovah and he'll help you to stay
On the right path he will help us to mend
This argument will eventually come to an end

"I JUST WANT A FRIEND"

I just want a friend
Right by my side
I just want a friend
That is very kind

One that treats me with respect
Never abandons and never neglects

With Jehovah's day drawing near
I need a friend when I shed a tear

Please help me out to face each test
Then our God will do the rest

Each of us will hug each other
In God's new world we'll stick together

I'm glad that I found a friend like you
To be there for me and to make it through

Don't worry about all the trying times
Because in the end we'll be just fine

I need a friend like you always
To always say it'll be okay

So don't look down with fear in your heart
Just hold on tight and have a part

With willingness and peace of mind
My dear friend we'll be just fine

With tears of joy we will always mend
Please stay with me and be my friend

"MAKE OUR FAITH STRONGER"

Make our faith stronger every day
For we need strength and to always pray

From our heart our faith will grow
In the end Jehovah knows

How to help us when we're in need
We don't have to hide behind a tree

If we have strong faith we'll make it through
That's because we wanted to

Love Jehovah, keep holding on
He'll be your shield from now on

He will shield us from the storm
He will be there when we weep and mourn

For we always keep standing tall
He will help us through it all

So because his day is near
Our faith will grow and shatter our tear

Make our faith stronger I'm down on my knee
For this will help you and me

Never forget me and always depend
I'll always have faith in you as my friend

"DO NOT BE AFRAID"

Do not be afraid
For I am with you
Do not be afraid
Yes, I will help you

From the darkest depths
I'll pull you through
Do not be afraid
I will help you

For everything will be alright
I will be your shining light

Never again will you tremble in fear
I, Jehovah am drawing you near

Do not be afraid for I am your rock
Your shield of protection to gather my flock

Do not be afraid I'm always with you
No matter what happens I'll carry you through

Just remember it is you I will bless
I will hold on to you
With me right hand of righteousness

"HOPE IN JEHOVAH"

Hope in Jehovah

And trust in him

For he will make us live again

From every moment that we live

Our heart of purpose moves us to give

Hope in Jehovah

And never weep

For his reminders we always keep

In this time of great despair

Look to him with Godly fear

Never knowing what will come our way

With joy of heart we will gladly say

Hope in Jehovah

With all our heart

We will make a brand new start

To Jehovah we will begin anew

In the paradise with me and you

Never looking back behind

Jehovah will give you peace of mind

Hope in Jehovah

And play your part

Be courageous and strong of heart

"NO MORE DEATH"

No more death
We look forward to see
Our faithful friends
Jehovah needs

We look to him
For love during this trying time
Please strengthen me
During this hard time

We know that these ones are just sleeping in death
Jehovah will awaken these ones
As they sing out with every grateful breath

Dear friends of Jehovah keep holding on
For we know that it won't be too long

Till Jehovah will settle all things
We look forward to the joy that happiness brings

No matter what happens to us if we die
Jehovah will give life to us in the future paradise

Always look forward to what Jehovah will give
We really long for the time when we will live

Forever on earth with joy from above
We will be happy as long as we love

"HE WILL CALL, THE DEAD WILL RISE"

He will call, the dead will rise
They were righteous before God's eyes

He will call, instead of sighing
Our loved ones are no longer dying

Because of him we stand up and yearn
For the day when we teach and learn

About the future that will come
Jehovah's will on earth is done

He will call, the dead will rise
This will come as no surprise

These faithful ones we have in our heart
To Jehovah we praise and begin a new start

He will call, and they will answer him
For they will live again

For the time will come when all sickness is gone
Nobody will say: "Hey, what's wrong?"

He will call, the dead will rise
Each one will live, keep your eyes on the prize

He will cherish these ones that will come to our aid
For the righteous and faithful He will rightfully save

As long as we do what is right in Jehovah's eyes
He will give us everlasting life!

"FLEE FROM THIS WORLD"

Flee from this world
It brings so much fear
Flee from this world
For God's day is near

Wake up and smile
With heartfelt affection
Why does this world
Create so much affliction?

Flee from this world
And never look back
For Satan will want
Something you lack

Flee from this world
And always rejoice
Lift up your head
And sing with your voice

Flee from this world
With heartfelt desire
Satan's world will soon be retired

"COME TO ME WHEN I'M DEPRESSED"

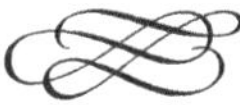

Come to me when I'm depressed
Because I feel really stressed

This sinful world is such a mess
Jehovah God, it's you he'll bless

Everything that comes our way
Peace of mind will fill our day

Come to me when I'm downhearted
I want to finish what we started

To hear your thoughts as I pray to you
My God Jehovah I hear you too

In your Word I look for strength
Instead of sorrow, instead of pain

Come to me when I'm depressed
Anxious thoughts fill my mind with stress

In God's new world these will go away
Happy thoughts I will always say

Thank Jehovah, he wants to help me
To be a part of his family

Come to me when I'm depressed
Jehovah will take away my stress

I look to him when I'm feeling down
I trust in him to lift my frown

No matter what I seem to go through
He will always be there for you

"TEARDROPS"

Teardrops fall when I am sad
Nobody knows that I feel bad

To speak from my heart
And to think where to start

I try my best to never look back
But happiness lingers, yet good things I lack

Teardrops are falling all over the place
With kind words, sadness I'll replace

I'm eager to stand up on my feet
These teardrops I'm determined to defeat

Jehovah will help me get rid of it all
He'll never let another teardrop fall

"GODLY FEAR"

With Godly fear we need to display
For thoughts of peace will come our way

Godly fear moves us to act
Trust in Jehovah for that's a fact

He'll build us up when he is near
He'll help us display Godly Fear

For he works hard to teach us good news
For this wicked world is almost through

Godly fear and hope we will see
It won't just be a fantasy

For with Godly fear we call to you
Asking what you want me to do

To prove to you that I have real hope
In this world you help me to cope

Every day with heartfelt praise
You will teach me in so many ways

I look forward to seeing your day drawing near
For I will always display Godly fear

Thank you Jehovah
For things that you give
Enjoyment of life and the life that we live

You take care of us when things don't go our way
Thoughtful words and actions we kindly display

Thank you Jehovah
In our time of need
We hope in you always your sheep you will lead

In the new world things will get much better
No more disasters and no more bad weather

Thank you Jehovah
In all that you do
We find in our heart to prove you are true

Everyday you will rightfully say
There's nothing to fear it will all be okay

Thank you Jehovah
My prayer came to an end
Through these hard times my heart you will mend
That's all for now
Through your Son Jesus
I say Amen!

"RISE UP"

Rise up
From the dark
Rise up
Don't go far

Rise up
When you're scared
Rise up
Be aware

Rise up
Never wonder
Rise up
God's Word we ponder

Rise up
Never frown
Rise up
From the ground

Jehovah will save you
He's always around
Rise up
From your fears
Rise up
He will care

Rise up
See the stars
No matter where you are

Jehovah is happy and always aware
Jehovah is happy to see you are there

"MEDITATE ON GOD'S WORD"

Meditate on God's Word
We are thankful for what we've heard

When we read we can relate
Things that people demonstrate

Meditate it means our life
Choosing what is wrong or right

This can always mean good news
It can always pull us through

Anyway to get inspired
Prove that Satan is a liar

Meditate we faithfully see
In God's new world eternally

Never knowing what's in store
We will praise you more and more

Meditate to daily feed
This is what we really need

Meditate on God's Word now
This will always lift our frown

We need his Word to keep on going
Jehovah God is wise, all knowing

Meditate to feed the mind
It will help us to be kind

Finding treasures everyday
Everything will be okay

"LOVE FROM THE HEART"

Love from the heart
That's where we will start

To treat each other with love
That comes from above

Love from the heart
We each play our part

To comfort and dwell
And to treat others well

Never with harsh or even with hate
We need to be kind for this is our fate

Love from the heart and never forget
All of our brothers and sisters we've met

Love from the heart for this will be true
I love every single one of you!

"ONE DAY AT A TIME"

Just take one day at a time
Don't worry too much for things will be fine

Things are so rough when I am alone
Whenever I knock there is no one home

The feel of despair when I'm always weak
Jehovah will help me his Word I will seek

One day at a time
Let's always be kind

No matter If love will get harder to find
Just take one more step

Yes, this can be true
I really want to be better in helping me and you

Let's take one day at a time
For when things get so hard

Jehovah will make everything fine

Let's always keep praying together
For our hearts to mend
This wicked world will eventually come to an end!

"DEEP DESPAIR"

Deep despair
I always fear
Deep despair
Is everywhere

I need help
To make it through
Jehovah please help
Me and you

From this world
That we live
Please take my hand
And forgive

Everything I've said to you
This Deep despair
Affects me and you

Deep despair

Just go away
I will want to pray all day

For Jehovah to help me out
So that I don't have to weep and pout

Deep despair
Will disappear
Peace will eventually be everywhere

"THERE FOR YOU"

I will always be there for you
To pick you up and to pull you through

I will always be your shining star
Jehovah your God is not very far

Look up to the heavens with pure delight
Everything will be alright

No matter what happens to you today
Everything will be okay

The storm is coming, yes, this I know
I'm not sure where I want to go

In this time during deep despair
I know you'll always be right there

I know you'll always be there for me
Jehovah God you help me to see

Through the troubles I deeply face
All anxiety I need to erase

I will always be there for you
Never doubting what you can do

Help me Jehovah I'm begging you please
I'm looking for answers I'm down on my knees

For you to take action for this I will show
Everything you've told me, yes, this I know

I've been wondering what you will do
I know you will say, I'll be there for you

"JESUS' SACRIFICE"

We're gathered together
On Nisan fourteen
The death of God's Son
And what it will always mean

We have great love forever
This we can always tell
Jesus' sacrifice
Will make everyone well

The bread on the table
Stands for Jesus' body
The wine stands for his blood
These have special meaning

For we keep this occasion
Close to us from the start
This love is so special
It is close to our heart

We're gathered together
For this special event
The wrong things we've done
From our sins we repent

For we honor your Son
He gave his life
For everyone

Let's always be thankful
This we can see
Keep doing this in remembrance of me

"EVERYWHERE"

Everywhere
You'll see it done
When you see the new world come

Everywhere
You'll see us smile
Since we haven't for a while

Everywhere
We need to rest
Cause we always tried our best

Everywhere
We'll see no crime
When each human will be kind

Everywhere
When peace abounds
Jehovah will always be around

Everywhere
We see each other
No one will bother one another

Everywhere
It seems to me
Everlasting life will bring

Everywhere
Thanks to our God above
The whole earth will be filled with love

"PREACH"

We need to preach
And we need to teach

The things that we find
To help others to be kind

We need to preach
To help others reach

Goals in their life
To distinguish what's right

We need other to
Help them pull through

Make changes so we can
Offer a helping hand

We need to preach

For it means our life

So we can obtain
Everlasting life

"TEARS OF JOY"

Tears of joy
Will come my way
Everything will be okay

Through the dark and through the night
Everything will be alright

Tears of joy
I'll wake up and see
My whole united family

On the earth when I know I can
Always take Jehovah's hand

Tears of joy
This shout of praise
Everyone will be amazed

Seeing the dead ones come to life
We'll have everlasting life

Tears of joy
We proudly cherish
No one on the earth will perish

This will come So very soon
I look forward to seeing you!

"WE NEED LOVE"

We need love
To make things better
We need love
As long as we're together

We need love
No more pain
Act like Abel and don't act like Cain

We need love
This we will know
We need love
Because Jehovah says so

This will make things better for me
Happiness I would like to see

We need love
All over the place
I want to see your happy face

We need love
Yes, this will come true
No more wickedness
For me and you

"JEHOVAH, JEHOVAH"

Jehovah, Jehovah
I stand up and see
Your Word, the Bible will come to me

I look at it with joy and delight
Now I know how to do what is right

Jehovah, Jehovah
I feel this desire
To read your Word and to get inspired

I know this reading will come to my aid
Praising you with everything that you've made

Jehovah, Jehovah
Yes, that is your name
We shouldn't look at humans
With honor and fame

I need to keep reading your Word
Everyday and every night
So that I will be able to come to your light

"DON'T BE SAD, DON'T FROWN"

Don't be sad and don't frown
I'll pull you up when you're feeling down

I know you're going through a lot
I'll give you everything I've got

Don't be sad when things are rough
I will always pull you up

From this world that we live in
I want to see you again

Don't be sad and don't frown
I will always be around

To lift you up and hold your hand
I will help you understand

Please help me to stay close to you
In every single thing I do

"BE DETERMINED"

Be determined to obey
Everything will be okay

Be determined I can stand
I will do everything I can

Be determined and be strong
Be determined to go on

Be determined to make things right
The new world is in our sight

Be determined never fear
For I will wipe out every tear

Be determined to carry on
I will always make you strong

Be determined always hope

Never worry always cope

For the new world is in our sight
Everything will be alright

"WE MISS ALL OF YOU"

These are hard times that we live in
Right now it's hard to stand

Time and time again
It's hard to understand
We just can't wait to see you again

We miss you
We send you all our love
Jehovah will make things better
As long as we stick together

We miss all of you
Soon we will all live forever
With no more pain and no more tears
And no disease that cause us to fear

We need hope from above
To nourish us with true love

Please understand how we feel
We have this hope that is real
I feel we can make it through
Because we miss all of you!

"COMFORT"

We all need comfort at times
During these critical times

We all feel like we need someone who cares
Every time that we're scared

Jehovah our God
You give us the comfort we need
Through hard times
Through sad times
It's you that cares for me

"DON'T GIVE UP"

Don't give up
Let Jehovah guide you
Don't give up
You know what you have to do

Don't give up
In doing what's good
Don't give up
Preparing spiritual food

Don't give up
And don't give in
Jehovah will make you happy again

Don't give up
When you face a trial
Don't give up
And give me a smile

Don't give up

It's plain to see
Don't give up
On you and me

Don't give up
It's been a while
Don't give up
When you're in denial

Don't give up
This we can depend
Don't give up
On you my friend

"THERE'S NOBODY ELSE"

There's nobody else
That I can rely on
There's nobody else
That can make me strong

There's nobody else
That can quench my thirst
I really want to put your Kingdom first

There's nobody else
That I can rely
There's nobody else
Who is there when I cry

There's nobody else
When I turn to you
There's nobody else
That I rely on but you

"STAND UP, STAND FIRM"

Stand up, stand firm
Show me what I need to learn

I need knowledge in my life
Conquering the darkness with the light

Stand firm, be bold
This is what we're always told

Everything that we desire
When no human will expire

Stand up, show love
Always to our God above

We have tender affection for all
Even if we're big or small

Stand firm, show zeal
We believe that you are real

Please show me that you are there
I know that you really care

Everything that you have made
When everything will be okay

Then I'll be there all the time
When everyone is feeling fine

Lift me up and stand firm
This is what I really yearn

"NEW WORLD"

We need the new world to come
Shining down on everyone

When the dead will come to life
When there's no more hateful strife

We need the new world to come
Enjoying life with everyone

No more pain and no more crime
When everything will be just fine

Walking out the door with joy
Everyone will be employed

We need the new world to come
When God's will on earth is done

Every time and everyway
We'll do things Jehovah's way

In the new world we will stay
Even if we have to pray

For we need a peaceful world
Even if we're a boy or a girl

We need the new world to come
This will bring blessings to everyone

Never having to be scared
To pet a lion or a bear

These are things that we will see
Everlasting life will bring

"NOW"

Now we need to be inspired
Keep learning what God requires

Now we need to preach constantly
Keep moving forward with constancy

Now we need to keep pushing through
In every single thing we do

Now we need to stand our ground
With our enemies around

They would like to weaken us
Draw close to God this is a must

Now's the time keep holding on
He will always make you strong

In this time we need you here
Whenever you stand right there

Now we need to feel this way
Pray to God, it'll be okay

Now we need to keep on trying
This whole world is slowly dying

We keep pushing through together
We can't wait to live forever

Now's the time to readjust
Our own life this is a must

To see what God will have in store
We will love him more and more

"IT TAKES FAITH"

It takes faith
Like that of Abel
Let's not feed on Satan's table

It's takes faith
Like that of Job
Things that God already knows

It takes faith
Like that of Abram
For God's righteous world will come

It takes faith
When we read God's Word
Even with each word we've heard

Faith grows stronger everyday
When we do things Jehovah's way

It takes faith

To understand
These faithful people take a stand

For Jehovah we endure
Never knowing if we're sure

It takes faith
To know what's best
When we always face each test

Under God's own sovereignty
This will help you and me

"JEHOVAH CAN"

Jehovah can
Create man
With his mighty righteous hand

Jehovah can
Make us stand
To his future promised land

Jehovah can
Make us strong
Even if he knows what's wrong

Jehovah can
And will be there
Even if we have this type of fear

Jehovah can
Help us out
Even if we weep and pout

Jehovah can
Bless our faith
As long as we follow his righteous ways

Jehovah can
And will defend
Everyone until the end!

"IN THE END"

In the end
It's so hard for me
To keep on moving spiritually

In the end
We need you
To keep on strengthening me and you

In the end
I look ahead
When Jehovah will raise the dead

In the end
We have no fear
Cause Jehovah is always near

In the end
We face tests
We know that we've tried our best

In the end
Jehovah knows
Which way we need to go

In the end
We look to you
We know that you're always true

ABOUT THE AUTHOR

My name is Adam Schroeder.

I have low-spectrum Autism and I also have a learning disability. But even with this I still strive to do my best in whatever I do. During my lifetime it has been a struggle. I did public performances when I was in school. I played the piano and I did the yo-yo. Now I am excited to dive into the wonderful world of poetry to tackle this fine art of words that have a lot of meaning behind them, especially when people out there are struggling like I did.

I am pleased to share my talent with everyone who reads this book. I really care about the impact the world has on people today, so I hope with strong conviction that my poems will ensure everyone with true satisfaction and certainty as we all strive to do our best in this world, come what may!

Sincerely,

Adam Schroeder